Content

Hi I'm Super Wormy! Can you spot me helping on each page?

Welcome to Super Medics

We are here to guide you through how to help someone who is unwell or injured. Learning how to provide first aid is a valuable skill that could help save a person's life. **First aid** is the initial help given to an unwell or injured person prior to professional help arriving.

Have you ever helped someone by giving first aid, or maybe called 999 for an ambulance?

(Don't forget to spot Super Wormy on each page!)

First Aid Kits

First aid kits contain useful items to help an unwell or injured person.

Do you know where your nearest first aid kit is?

Ask an adult to help you match the contents of your family first aid kit to the check list below.

Can you see the expiry dates on your kit at home?

Remember that first aid kits should not contain any tablets or medications.

 **Triangular Bandages**

  Bandages

  Gloves

 **Antiseptic Wipes**

  Plasters

  **Safety Pins**

 **Sterile Water**

 Instructions

The latest recommendations on what should be included in your first aid kit can be found at www.super-medics.com/first-aid-kits

Calling an Ambulance

You can call 999 or 112 from any phone in the UK to contact the emergency services; Ambulance, Fire or Police.

What they need to know

When calling for an ambulance it is important to provide as many details as possible about what has happened.

❀ Is the person breathing?

❀ Where are you?

❀ What has happened?

Don't worry if you are unsure what to say, the call taker will guide you.

Remember to stay calm, take a deep breath and reassure the unwell or injured person.

How to Help an Unwell or Injured Person

When helping someone who is unwell or injured it is important to follow DRS ABC.

Danger

Response

Shout for help

Airway

Breathing

CPR

ALWAYS KEEP YOURSELF SAFE

Before we can help someone who is unwell or injured we must check for dangers.

- Is it **safe** for me to help?
- Is the person in any further **danger**?
- Could anyone else get **hurt** too?

See how many dangers you can spot on this page.

Response

RESPONSE CHECK

Once it is safe to help, we need to check how responsive the person is.

- ❀ Are they **alert**?
- ❀ Do they respond to your **voice**?
- ❀ If not, do they react if you gently put **pressure** on their shoulders?
- ❀ If not, they are **unresponsive**.

Shout for help

SHOUT LOUD AND CLEAR

It is important to get help as soon as possible.

Shout '**Help**' out loud to get someone's attention and ask them to call an ambulance.

If you are on your own you may need to call **999** yourself and ask for an ambulance.

If you can, put the phone on loud speaker so the call taker can guide you while you help the person.

Airway

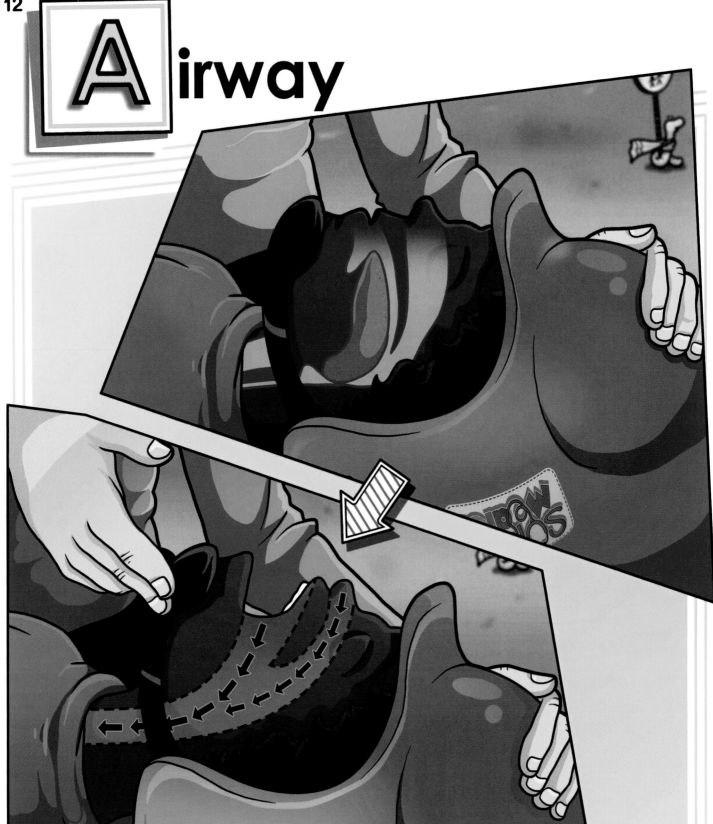

IS THEIR AIRWAY OPEN?

If the person is unresponsive we need to gently open their airway. Place one hand on their head and two fingers under their chin. Now gently tilt their head back. This will help to stop the tongue from blocking their airway.

Note: If the person is wearing a safety helmet **leave it on** and tell the 999 call taker.

Breathing

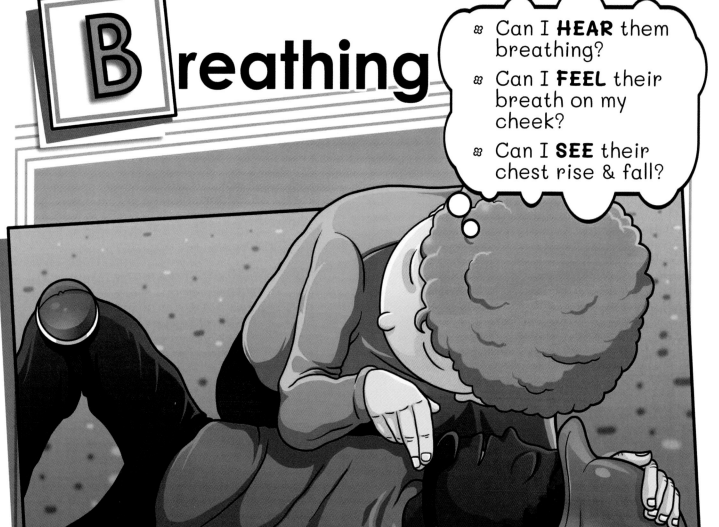

- Can I **HEAR** them breathing?
- Can I **FEEL** their breath on my cheek?
- Can I **SEE** their chest rise & fall?

ARE THEY BREATHING?

Now we need to check the persons breathing. Whilst holding their airway open, put your cheek near their nose and mouth while looking at their chest for up to 10 seconds.

Are they breathing normally, are they breathing at all or are there some infrequent noises ('Zombie-like' breaths)?

If they are **not breathing normally** we need to start CPR (Go to pages 14 & 15 for adults or 18 & 19 for babies and children).

If they are **breathing normally** put them in the recovery position (Go to page 20).

CPR

If someone is not breathing normally, we need to start CPR as soon as possible.

① Perform 30 chest compressions

Kneel by the side of the person.

Place the heel of one hand in the centre of their chest.

Place the heel of your other hand on top of the first hand.

Interlock your fingers.

Keep your arms straight with your shoulders above your hands.

Press down **hard and fast** to 1/3 of the depth of the chest (normally 5-6 cm for an adult sized person).

After each compression, make sure you release all pressure on the chest.

Repeat at a rate of 2 a second (100—120 compressions per minute).

④ Keep Going

Keep doing 30 compressions and then 2 breaths until the person wakes up, someone takes over, or you are too tired to carry on.

Tom's helpful hint

If your mouth is too small to fit over theirs, try closing their mouth and blow through their nose instead!

③

Perform 2 rescue breaths

Take a normal breath and blow steadily into the mouth for 1 second, while watching the chest rise.

Take another breath and repeat a second time.

② Open the airway
(as shown on page 12).

Pinch the soft part of the nose while opening the person's mouth.

Defibrillators (AED)

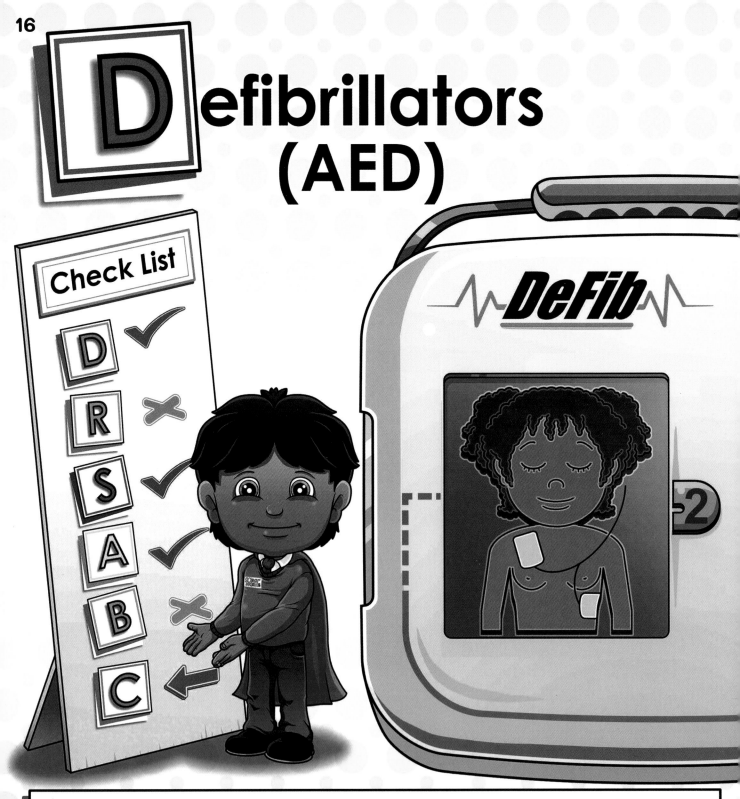

Check List

D ✓
R ✗
S ✓
A ✓
B ✗
C

An Automatic External Defibrillator (AED) is a life saving device used on unresponsive patients that are NOT breathing normally.

They are safe and very easy to use, but remember not to touch the patient when it tells you not to.

An AED will decide if the heart needs an electric shock to help it beat properly and will ask you to push the 🔘 shock button if it is needed.

The AED's sticky pads show you where to place them straight onto the person's skin (see page 18 & 19 for use on a baby or child).

AED PADS

HOW TO USE

1 **Switch on** the AED.

2 **Attach the pads** on the person's bare chest as shown (remove their clothing and dry their skin if required).

3 **Listen** to instructions from the AED.

4 **Do not touch the person** while the AED is checking the rhythm.

5 If required **push the ⚡ shock button** as directed.

6 Immediately **restart CPR** (30 compressions and then 2 breaths).

7 **Continue** as directed by the voice/visual prompts.

ON/OFF

Shock button

Remember to shout for help and make sure an ambulance is on its way.

Do you know where your nearest AED is?

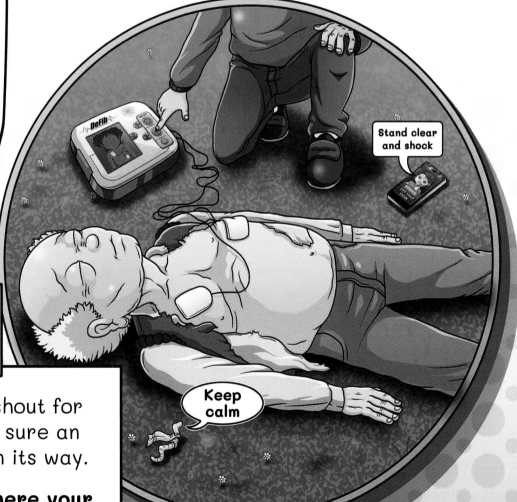

Stand clear and shock

Keep calm

Baby and Child CPR

For an unresponsive baby or child who is **not breathing normally**, we need to do CPR slightly differently.

① OPEN THE AIRWAY

Opening an airway on a baby or child is the same as an adult.

Be careful not to push too hard under the chin.

For a baby, having a small blanket or jumper under the shoulders is helpful.

② PERFORM RESCUE BREATHS

Initially, **give 5 breaths** (once only before any chest compressions).

If their mouth is very small, you can **breathe over the nose and mouth** together.

Ensure you get a small chest rise (and fall). Don't breathe too hard!

All further rescue breaths are given as **2 breaths**.

If an AED is available, make sure that it is applied and turned on as soon as possible. For babies and children **the pads stick to their front and back** (as below). If the pads are close to touching, the child is too small and the pads must be removed. Continue CPR through-out and time off the chest should be minimised.
Don't touch them when the AED is analysing or shocking!

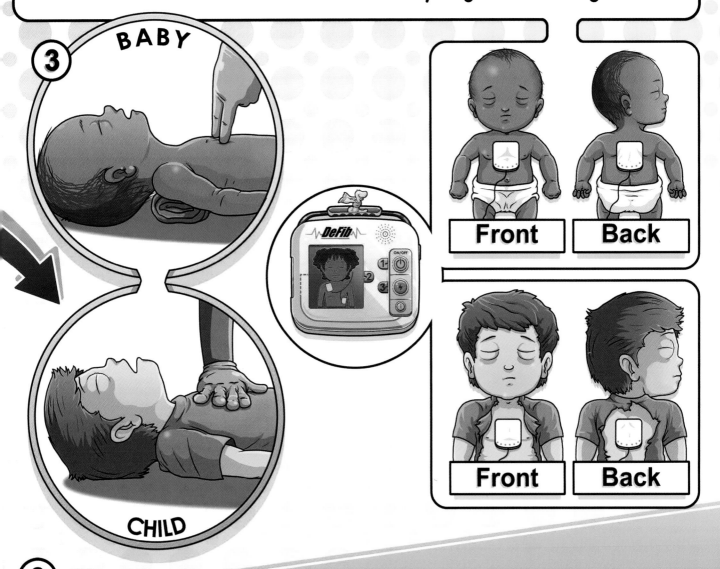

BABY

③

CHILD

Front Back

Front Back

③

PERFORM 30 CHEST COMPRESSIONS

As for adult CPR, carry out **30 chest compressions in the centre of the chest** using 2 fingers for babies, or 1 hand for a child.

Keep going - 30 compressions and then 2 breaths until the person wakes up, someone takes over or you are too tired to carry on.

ALWAYS CALL 999 IF CPR IS HAPPENING

Make sure help is on the way and an ambulance is called urgently. Switch your phone onto loud speaker, so you can talk to the call taker while helping the person.

Recovery Position

We use the recovery position to help keep the airway open and prevent choking (in case they are sick or have food in their mouth). If you think a person may have a back injury, do not attempt to move them until the emergency services arrive.

You should suspect a back injury if the person:

- Has been involved in an accident such as a fall from height or has been struck directly in the back, or
- Complains of severe pain in their neck or back, or
- Won't move their neck, or
- Feels weak, numb or they can't move their arms or legs.

Keep an eye on them and be prepared to start CPR if the person stops breathing normally (pages 14 & 15).

Arm at right angle

1

Kneel next to the person and put their arm closest to you at a right angle.

If they are wearing glasses, remove them and place in their hand.

Hand + knee movement

2

Bring their other arm across the chest, and hold the back of the hand against the patient's cheek nearest to you. With your other hand, hold the far leg just above the knee and pull it up (keep their foot on the ground).

Body roll

3

Now, while keeping hold of their hand, pull on the far leg to roll the person onto their side towards you.

Leg + airway adjust

4

Adjust their upper leg so that it is at a right angle.

Tilt the head back slightly to make sure that their airway is open.

Monitor

5

Stay with the person until the ambulance arrives and monitor to make sure they are breathing normally.

Choking: Children & Adults

Choking can happen when something like food or a toy gets stuck in the airway. This can stop the air from getting to the lungs and is a medical emergency. They may be holding their neck, look a different colour and be very worried. To help;

1. Ask the person, "**Are you choking?**".

2. If they are choking, ask them, "**Can you cough?**".

3. If they can cough, encourage them to continue coughing and **get help.**

If the person can't cough then follow the steps below...

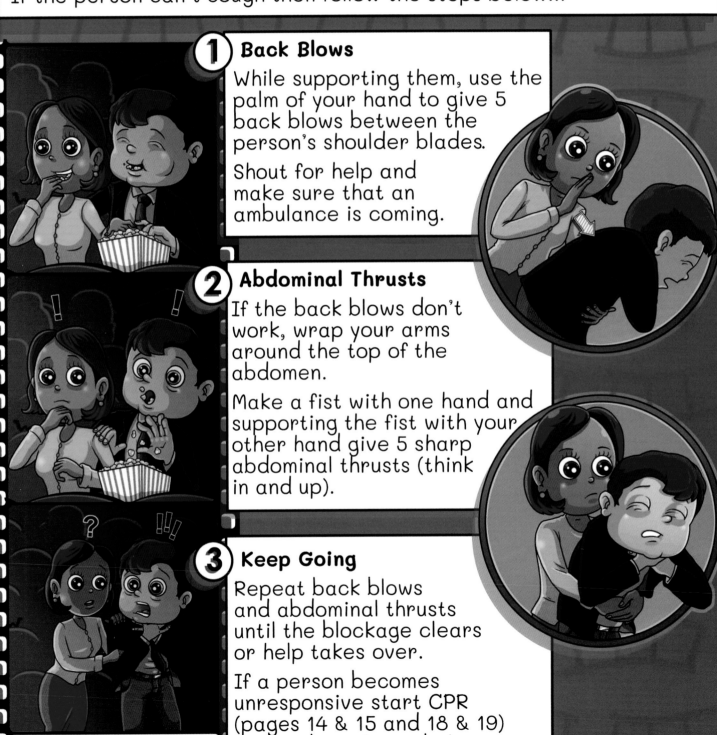

1 Back Blows

While supporting them, use the palm of your hand to give 5 back blows between the person's shoulder blades.

Shout for help and make sure that an ambulance is coming.

2 Abdominal Thrusts

If the back blows don't work, wrap your arms around the top of the abdomen.

Make a fist with one hand and supporting the fist with your other hand give 5 sharp abdominal thrusts (think in and up).

3 Keep Going

Repeat back blows and abdominal thrusts until the blockage clears or help takes over.

If a person becomes unresponsive start CPR (pages 14 & 15 and 18 & 19) and update the ambulance.

Choking: Babies

If a baby starts choking, like children and adults they may change colour and will be distressed. Shout for help and get an ambulance. Turn the baby **face down across your lap** in a head-downwards position with their head supported (so gravity can help).

Give **5 back blows between their shoulder blades**, then check to see if the blockage has cleared. If not, turn the baby over and using 2 fingers, give **5 chest thrusts** (a bit like chest compressions but sharper and slower).

Repeat the back blows and chest thrusts until they recover or someone takes over. If they become unresponsive **start CPR** as per pages 18 & 19 and update the ambulance.

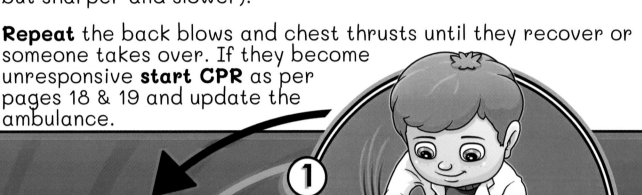

Give the baby **5 back blows.**

If the baby is still choking give **5 chest thrusts**.

Repeat back blows and chest thrusts until the baby recovers or help takes over.

If they become unresponsive update the ambulance service and **start CPR** (pages 18 & 19).

The Heart

The heart is responsible for pumping blood around our bodies. It is located near the centre of our chest and is protected by the rib cage.

The heart has 4 chambers and beats rhythmically, pumping deoxygenated blood to the lungs (where it is refuelled with oxygen) and freshly oxygenated blood around the body. Arteries carry blood away from the heart, capillaries (small blood vessels) deliver the oxygen to our cells and veins return blood to the heart.

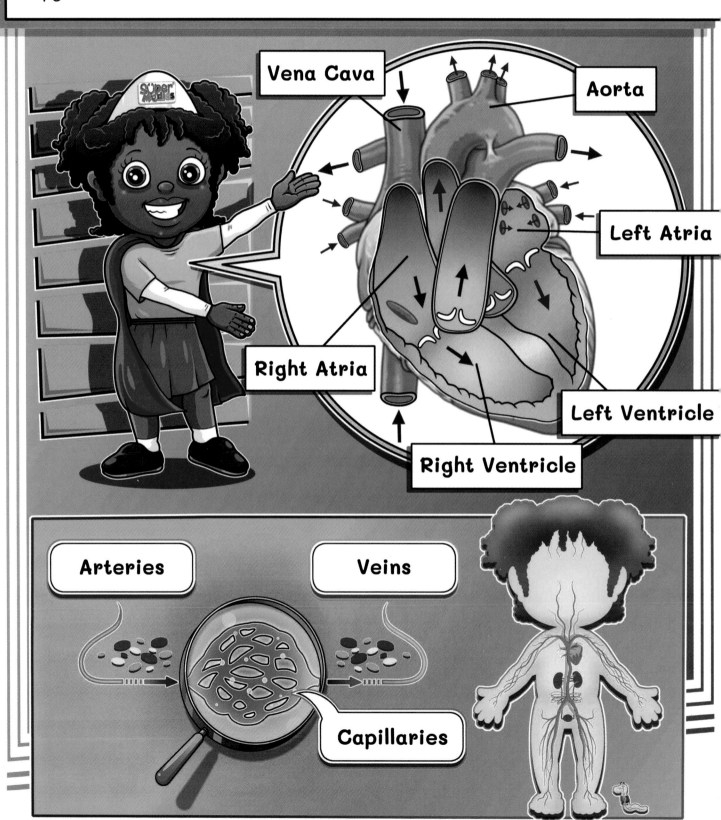

Heart Attack

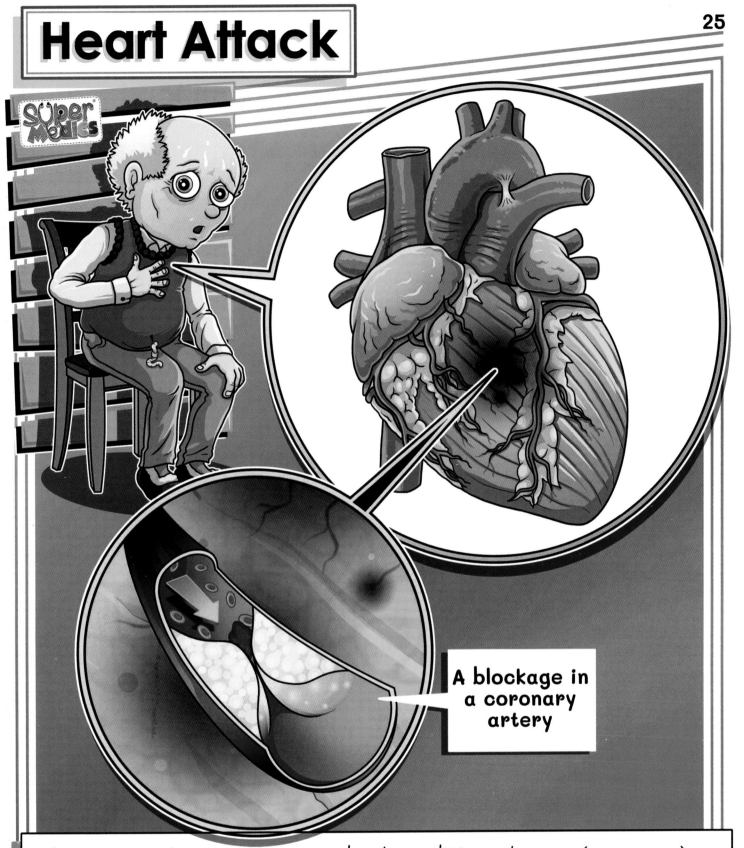

A blockage in a coronary artery

A heart attack is a serious medical condition where a (coronary) artery within the heart becomes blocked. This prevents adequate blood flow to the heart, and without help that part of the heart may die. Symptoms can include chest pain, sweating, dizziness, shortness of breath, looking poorly and tingling in the arms. If you think someone is having a heart attack, make them comfortable, get them to sit on the floor and call 999.

If they become unresponsive and stop breathing normally, start CPR (pages 14 & 15 and 18 & 19), update the ambulance and shout for help for somebody to bring the nearest AED to you.

Lungs

Our lungs are incredible, breathing in and out, day and night without us even thinking about them.

Our lungs are responsible for providing the oxygen our organs need to survive.

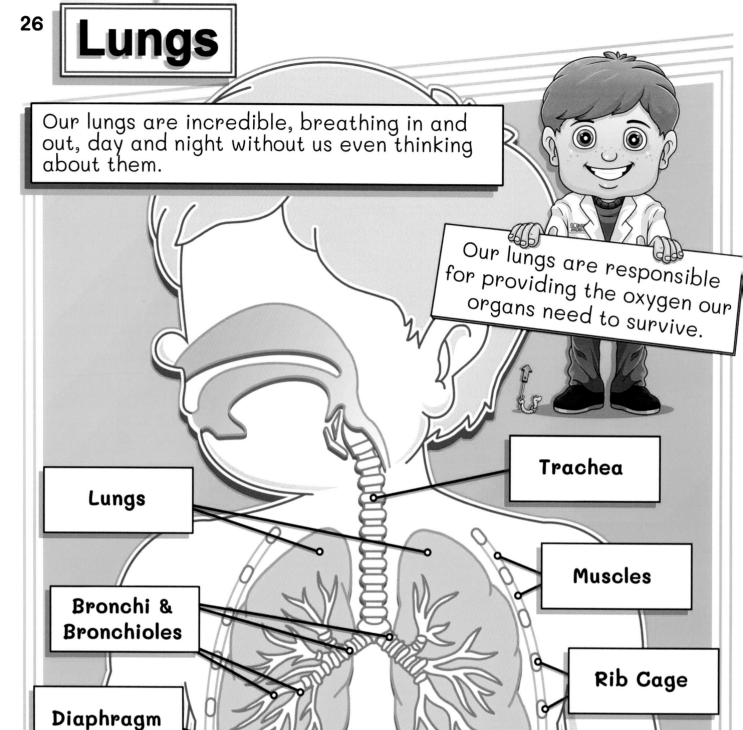

Trachea

Lungs

Muscles

Bronchi & Bronchioles

Rib Cage

Diaphragm

The respiratory centre in our brain controls breathing to make sure that our cells get the oxygen they need and to eliminate carbon dioxide. The air we breathe contains oxygen which the cells in our bodies need to stay alive.

To breathe, the big muscle under our lungs known as the diaphragm (and some of its surrounding muscles) contracts. This makes the chest cavity bigger and pulls the air through our trachea (windpipe) and into our lungs (where gas exchange occurs). To breathe out, the diaphragm and the associated muscles relax, which allows the rib cage to fall back into place, pushing the air out. If somebody has breathing difficulties it can be serious if left untreated - you must get medical help urgently by calling 999.

Asthma

Asthma is a common long term medical condition that can affect children and adults. People suffering with asthma have very sensitive airways that can become narrow and tighten, making it hard to breathe. Their chest becomes tight and wheezy and their face may change colour, such as their lips turning blue. They are struggling to get oxygen into their lungs. It can be really scary for the person and the people around them.

When a person is diagnosed with asthma they may be given an inhaler. This can help them by relaxing their airways and allowing them to breathe more freely. If the person becomes unresponsive and is not breathing normally it is important to start CPR and update the ambulance straight away (pages 14 & 15 and 18 & 19).

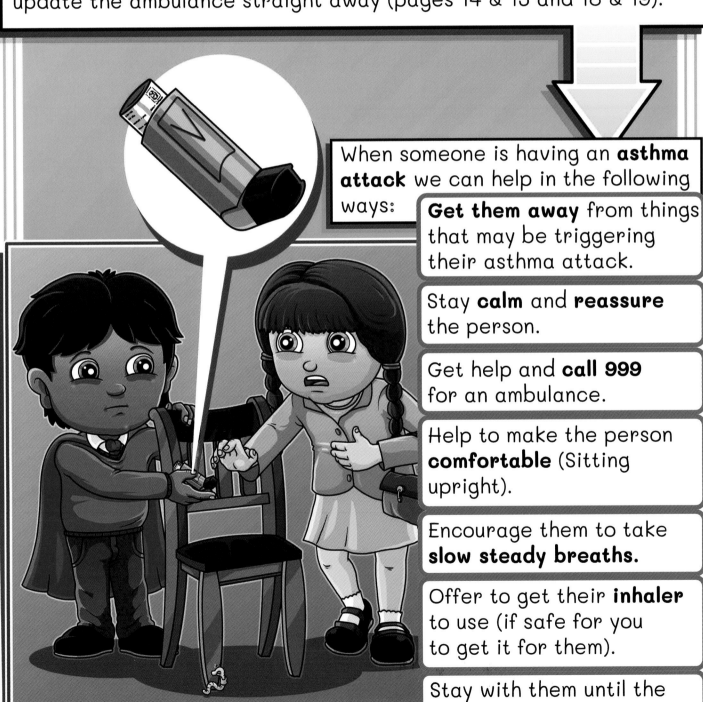

When someone is having an **asthma attack** we can help in the following ways:

Get them away from things that may be triggering their asthma attack.

Stay **calm** and **reassure** the person.

Get help and **call 999** for an ambulance.

Help to make the person **comfortable** (Sitting upright).

Encourage them to take **slow steady breaths.**

Offer to get their **inhaler** to use (if safe for you to get it for them).

Stay with them until the **ambulance** arrives.

Injuries

Blood

Blood transports oxygen and nutrients around the body via blood vessels (arteries, veins and capillaries). An injury to the body such as a cut, tear, puncture or bruise can cause blood to leak from these vessels and potentially leave the body. If an artery or vein is damaged the wound will bleed a lot and the person will need help urgently.

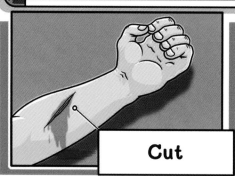

Cut

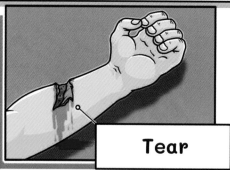

Tear

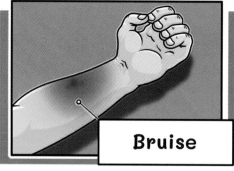

Bruise

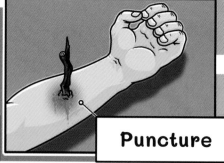

Puncture

Broken bones

Broken bones (fractures) can be very painful and need emergency care as soon as possible. There are many types of fractures including open, closed, complicated and green stick. If you suspect that someone has fractured a bone, they need to go to A & E for an X-ray and immediate medical care. Reassure the person and make them comfortable. Protect and dress the wound if it is open to reduce bleeding and infection.

X-ray

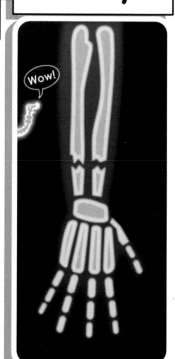

Treatment

When helping someone who is unwell or injured we follow DRS ABC. Are there any dangers? Is the person responsive? Have you shouted or called for help?

If they are talking to you, then their airway is open and they are breathing, so now we can take a look at any injuries.

⚘ What type of injuries are there?

⚘ Are they bleeding?

⚘ Is anything sticking out from the skin?

Ask the person if it's ok to help them.

Reassure the person and help to make them comfortable.

Lay them down if they feel dizzy and **treat for shock** (page 30).

If possible, wash hands and put **gloves** on.

Never remove anything sticking out of the wound!

Clean using bottled or cold tap water if available.

If it is an open wound then **bandage** as needed.

If still bleeding, apply **direct pressure** over the injury through the bandage (never push on anything sticking out, e.g. a stick).

☑ Gloves
☑ Mobile Phone
☑ Bandages
☑ Sterile Water
☑ Plasters
☑ Antiseptic Wipes

If someone is seriously hurt we must always call 999 for an ambulance

If the person becomes unresponsive, consider the recovery position (pages 20 & 21). If they stop breathing start CPR (pages 14 & 15 and 18 & 19), but make sure that the 999 call taker has been updated!

Burns

ARGH!!

Burns and scalds happen when the skin is exposed to extreme heat that damages the skin layers. They can be really painful and need first aid treatment straight away. **Remove the person from any danger** and take off jewellery or items around or below the burn (unless they are stuck). Now place the burn under **cool running water** for a minimum of **20 minutes**. Once cooled, ideally **cover the burn** with cling film (layer it across the burn, **do not wrap it** around as the burn may swell up) or if not available, apply a wet non-fluffy dressing. If needed, keep the person warm with a blanket. If they feel dizzy or unwell **treat them for shock** (see below). Make sure that adult help is on the way, as they may need to go to hospital.

Shock

Shock is a condition where there isn't enough oxygen reaching the body's organs and tissues. It can happen due to a number of reasons including severe burns, anaphylaxis and severe blood loss. Signs and symptoms include pale clammy skin, fast breathing, feeling weak, cold, dizzy and sick. To help a person with shock first **make sure you are both safe** and not in any danger. Encourage the person to **lie down, raise their legs** a little and support them (be careful of any injuries). **Keep them warm** and treat any injuries they may have. Make sure that adult help is on the way and **call 999** for an ambulance.

Generally Unwell & Sepsis

When someone is unwell it is important to **get advice and help from a medical professional**. Sometimes when we have an infection our body's immune system can go into **overdrive** and cause a reaction throughout the whole body. This can make us really sick and can cause an illness called **Sepsis**. Symptoms can be the same as other conditions (like the flu for example) making it difficult to spot. If you know someone who is poorly and are **unsure what to do**, there is a free helpline available (**NHS 111**). The friendly advisers can help you and transfer you to the 999 ambulance call centre if needed.

Sepsis is a **medical emergency.** Anyone who has it must go straight to hospital for urgent care.
Any kind of infection that is left untreated can lead to Sepsis, but it is treatable with **early recognition** and medical help. Signs and symptoms can include any number of the following conditions:

Sweaty or clammy skin

Feeling very poorly

Pale blotchy skin

Confusion & feeling sleepy

Difficulty breathing

Shivering or fever

Fast heart rate

Get help!

If someone is acting confused, not making sense or has difficulty breathing, get adult help and call 999 immediately.

Anaphylaxis

Allergic reactions are uncomfortable and often cause a rash on the skin, sneezing and itchy eyes. This happens when a person has been in contact with something that they are allergic to, for example being stung by a bee or eating nuts. **Anaphylaxis** is a **life threatening** allergic reaction that usually develops **suddenly and gets worse** very quickly as they develop airway and **breathing difficulties**.

Triggers can include

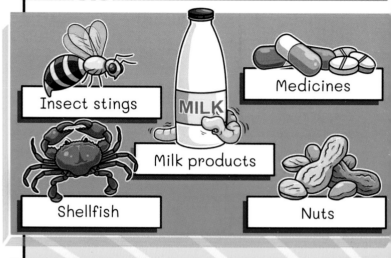

Insect stings

Milk products

Medicines

Shellfish

Nuts

Adrenaline Auto-Injector

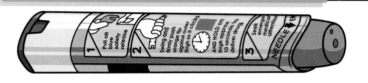

Symptoms can include

Swelling to face, eyes and mouth

Itchy skin

Difficulty breathing

People who are diagnosed with anaphylaxis may carry their medication in the form of an **adrenaline auto-injector** (such as an Epipen, Jext or Emerade pen). If they come into contact with one of their triggers and start feeling unwell they should use their auto injector straight away. To do this, **take the cap off** and **jab it in to their upper leg** through any clothing they are wearing. **Hold it firmly** in place for up to **10 seconds**, making sure that you follow the instructions on the injector. If you think someone is having an anaphylactic reaction help them to find their medicine, get help from an adult and **call 999** for an ambulance. If the person becomes unresponsive and stops breathing update the ambulance straight away and start CPR (pages 14 & 15 and 18 & 19).